Bath Knits

Bath Knits

30 PROJECTS MADE TO PAMPER

Mary Beth Temple

STACKPOLE BOOKS

Guilford, Connecticut

Published by Stackpole Books
An imprint of Globe Pequot

Distributed by National Book Network

We have made every effort to ensure the accuracy and completeness of these
instructions. We cannot, however, be responsible for human error, typographical
mistakes, or variations in individual work.

Copyright © 2017 by Mary Beth Temple
Cover design by Caroline M. Stover
Photography by Kimberly Brandt
Illustrations by Lindsey Stephens

Library of Congress Cataloging-in-Publication Data

Names: Temple, Mary Beth, author.
Title: Bath knits : 30 projects made to pamper / Mary Beth Temple.
Description: First edition. | Mechanicsburg, PA : Stackpole Books, 2016. |
  Includes index.
Identifiers: LCCN 2015047860 | ISBN 9780811716574 (pbk.)
Subjects: LCSH: Knitting--Patterns. | Bath towels. | Knit goods.
Classification: LCC TT825 .T415 2016 | DDC 746.43/2--dc23 LC record available at
http://lccn.loc.gov/2015047860

ISBN 978-0-8117-1657-4 (paperback)
ISBN 978-0-8117-6368-4 (e-book)

The paper used in this publication meets the minimum requirements of
American National Standard for Information Sciences—Permanence of Paper for
Printed Library Materials, ANSI/NISO Z39.48-1992.

Contents

Introduction

It's no secret that a lot of knitters like to make washcloths. They're quick, come in an endless variety of shapes and patterns, and can be as easy or challenging technique-wise as you wish to make them.

But in this book, I invite you to go deeper into your bathroom décor! Yes there are fabulous washcloth patterns but also so much more—everything you might want for your bathroom from towels to bathmats to art for the walls. Put your nail polish in a pretty lacquer tray with a knitted liner under the glass bottom. Get a pedicure in style in lace pedicure socks. There's even a chenille bathrobe to lounge in, with matching headband and slippers so you can primp for your busy day or night out in comfort.

While many of these projects can introduce you to new-to-you shapes or stitch patterns, none are particularly difficult to make. Work your way through these pages and emerge with both a new arsenal of knitters' tricks and a quick and affordable bathroom update!

Before You Begin

You may notice that the listed gauge for many of these projects calls for a smaller needle size than the yarn label might suggest. As a general rule, anything that's going to get wet is going to be knit at a very tight gauge to make sure the item doesn't pull out of shape in the water. Also note: Linens and cottons (which are especially well suited to these projects) are notoriously hard on your hands as you knit. Make sure to alternate these projects with others in your to-do list so you don't wear out your hands!

I have divided the book up into sections based on color and style, but there is no reason at all you can't take a project from any section of the book and change up the color to go where *you* want it to go! Make sure to look at all the sections before you decide which pieces will work best in your unique home.

The Naturals

Creams, tans, and silvers—colors found in nature—beautifully accent a country, rustic, or natural-styled bathroom. Textures rule, with the visual interest coming from the play of the stitching rather than any pops of bright color. Simple shapes, dense stitches, and subtle color combinations make these projects shine.

Tab-Top Towel

Guests or kids forever dropping your hand towels on the floor, where they lay in a damp heap? The two large buttons on this tab-top towel keep it on the towel bar where it belongs, and also add some visual punch.

Tip

When changing color for the center section between the garter stitch borders, remember to be consistent when picking up the new color (new color under old color, always) to make sure the join doesn't have gaps and is attractive on the wrong side of the work.

Finished Size

12³/₄" x 15" (32.5 x 38 cm), excluding tabs.

Materials

- 400 yd. (366 m) worsted weight #4 yarn, in two colors [shown in Premier Home Cotton Multis; 85% cotton, 15% polyester; 2.1 oz. (60 g), 105 yd. (96 m) per skein (A); and Premier Home Cotton Solids; 85% cotton, 15% polyester; 2.82 oz. (80 g), 140 yd. (128 m) per skein (B)]
  2 skeins #4421 Sahara Splash (A)
  1 skein #3802 Cream (B)
- U.S. size 5 (3.75 mm) knitting needles, or size needed to obtain gauge
- 2 two-holed buttons, 1³/₄" (4.5 cm)
- Tapestry needle

Gauge

17 sts and 26 rows in St st = 4" (10 cm)

Towel

Border

With A, cast on 54 sts with long-tail cast-on.
Knit 19 more rows for 10 garter stitch ridges.

Center Section

Row 1 (WS): K10, with B p34, with second strand of A k10.
Row 2 (RS): K10, with B k34, with A k10.
Rep Rows 1–2 until work measures 13" (33 cm) from cast-on edge, ending with a WS row. End off B and second strand of A.

Top Border

With A, knit 20 rows for 10 garter stitch ridges.

Tabs

Bind off 5, k9 more (10 sts on needle including 1 st from bind-off), bind off 24, k9 more, bind off 5. End off A.
Knit each tab separately with A until it measures 6¹/₂" (16.5 cm) from start of tab, ending with a WS row.

BUTTONHOLE

Row 1: K3, k2tog, ssk, k3—8 sts.
Rows 2–7: With separate strands of A, k4 with first strand, k4 with second strand.
Row 8: K4, cast on 2, k4—10 sts. End off second strand of A.
Rows 9–16: Knit.
Row 17: K2tog, knit until 2 sts remain, k2tog—8 sts.
Row 18: Knit.
Rows 19–22: Rep Rows 17–18 twice—4 sts after Row 21.
Row 23: K2tog twice—2 sts.
Bind off.

Finishing

Orient buttons vertically and sew them into place with the tapestry needle.
Weave in all ends.
Block if desired.

Exfoliating Washcloth

Small but mighty, use this thickly textured washcloth to help remove grime from your toddler or make-up from your face!

Tip
This stitch pattern is created in the same way as a cable, which is to say it's much easier than it looks! If you can complete a simple cable, you can make this washcloth as well.

Finished Size
6" x 6" (15 x 15 cm)

Materials
- 125 yd. (114 m) worsted weight #4 yarn [shown in Premier Home Cotton Solids; 85% cotton, 15% polyester; 2.82 oz. (80 g), 140 yd. (128 m) per skein] 1 skein #3802 Cream
- U.S. size 5 (3.75 mm) knitting needles, or size needed to obtain gauge
- Cable needle
- Tapestry needle

Gauge
26 sts and 28 rows in central pattern = 4" (10 cm)

Special Stitches
LC (left cross): Place 2 sts on cable needle, hold in front of work, knit 2 sts from left-hand needle, knit 2 sts from cable needle.
RC (right cross): Place 2 sts on cable needle, hold behind work, knit 2 sts from left-hand needle, knit 2 sts from cable needle.

Washcloth

Cast on 42 sts.
Row 1 (RS): Knit.
Row 2 and remaining WS rows until border: P4, k1, p32, k1, p4.
Row 3: K4, p1, k32, p1, k4.
Row 5: RC, p1, (LC, RC) 4 times, p1, RC.
Row 7: Rep Row 3.
Row 9: RC, p1, (RC, LC) 4 times, p1, RC.
Rows 10–12: Rep Rows 6–8.
Rep Rows 5–12 four times for pattern.
Next two rows: Knit.
Bind off.
Weave in ends.

Exfoliating Washcloth

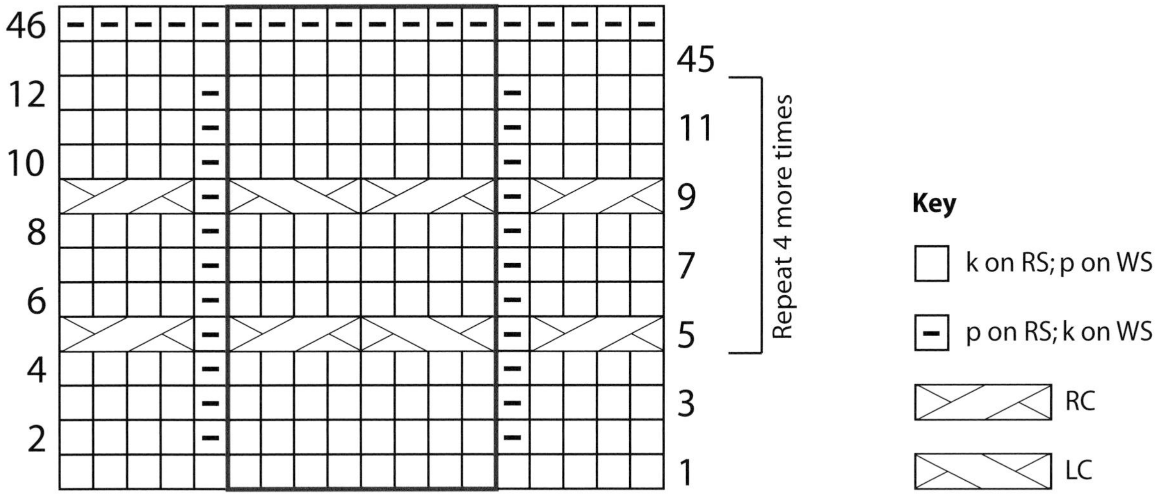
46
12
10
8
6
4
2
45
11
9
7
5
3
1
Repeat 4 more times
Key
k on RS; p on WS
p on RS; k on WS
RC
LC

Repeat marked in red

Felted Soap Cover

Rustic soap-on-a-rope! I've been seeing variations of these at sheep and wool festivals for years and wanted to include a pattern here. As you use the covered soap, the exterior felts (make sure you don't use superwash wool!) and shrinks. This one has an I-cord so you can hang it to dry between uses and the soap doesn't melt away too quickly.

Tip
These take hardly any wool at all to make and make great gifts! Use a long color repeat yarn like I did here and you will come up with all sorts of color combos while only using one skein of yarn.

Finished Size

To fit a bar of soap 2^1/$_4$" x 3^1/$_4$" (5.5 x 8.5 cm). Gauge is not
critical—just make sure your bar of soap fits in the bag.

Materials

- Approximately 40 yd. (36.5 m) chunky weight #5 wool
  yarn [shown in Plymouth Yarns Gina Chunky; 100%
  wool; 3.5 oz. (100 g), 131 yd. (120 m) per skein]
  1 skein #1014 Sunset
- U.S. size 8 (5 mm) double-pointed needles
- Stitch marker
- Bar of soap
- Tapestry needle

Soap Cover

Hold two DPNs next to each other and cast 11 sts onto
each (22 sts total) by using either a figure eight cast-on
or a standard long-tail cast-on, alternating needles
after every st cast on.

Set up to work in the round and mark beg of rnd.

Work 22 rnds St st (knit every row), or number of rows
needed to completely cover your bar of soap.

Insert soap into soap cover and close the top using
three-needle bind-off until 2 sts remain on each
needle for 4 sts total. There is one st on working
needle; k2tog using 1 st from each needle, twice.
There are 3 sts on right needle.

Work 8" (20.5 cm) of I-cord on these 3 sts. End off.

Finishing

With tapestry needle, whipstitch I-cord into a loop as
shown in photograph.

Weave in all ends.

Plush Bathmat

Who doesn't love to sink their toes into a thick, cushy bathmat when they step out of the tub or shower? Super bulky yarn held double with a simple-to-learn texture stitch means you can have this soft, washable bathmat finished in a couple of evenings.

Tip

It's simple to adjust the size of this bathmat: Either add or subtract an even number of stitches for the width, and add or subtract an even number of rows for the height.

Finished Size
28" x 20" (71 x 51 cm)

Materials
- 300 yd. (275 m) super bulky #6 yarn [shown in Plymouth Yarn Encore Mega; 75% acrylic, 25% wool; 3.5 oz. (100 g), 64 yd. (59 m) per skein] 5 skeins #0256
- U.S. size 15 (10 mm) knitting needles, or size needed to obtain gauge
- Tapestry needle

Gauge
4.5 sts and 6 rows in pattern st with yarn held double = 4" (10 cm)

Pattern Notes
- Yarn is held double throughout.

Special Stitches
K1b (knit 1 below): Insert right needle tip through st under the first st on the left needle, catching both that st and the one on the needle. Complete knit st and drop from left needle. It should not unravel.

Bathmat

Border
With yarn held double, cast on 35 sts with long-tail cast-on.
Knit 6 rows.

Pattern Section
Row 1 (RS): K4, k1b, *k1, k1b. Rep from * until 4 sts remain, k4.
Rows 2 and 4 (WS): Knit.
Row 3 (RS): K5, k1b, *k1, k1b. Rep from * across until 5 sts remain, k5.
Rep Rows 1–4 for pattern until work measures 18" (45.5 cm) or 2" (5 cm) less than desired finished height, ending with a Row 2.
Knit 4 more rows and bind off.

Finishing
Block if desired.
Weave in all ends.

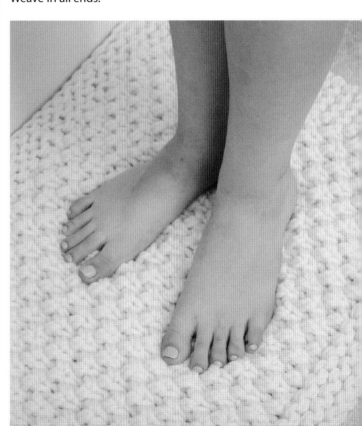

Lacy Mirror

While I wouldn't try to put on eyeliner when looking into it, this lace-covered mirror is a terrific accent piece for the bathroom wall. You can easily find a similar mirror at any craft chain store. All it took was a quick shot of clear lacquer and an hour of knitting and it was ready to assemble.

Tip

If you can't find the perfect mirror, simply insert a piece of aluminum sheeting or other reflective material in your favorite square picture frame.

Finished Size

Outer edge: 14" (35.5 cm) square

Mirror insert: 8" (20.5 cm) square

These are the measurements of the mirror I used, but you can easily adjust this pattern to your mirror's dimensions.

Materials

- Approximately 50 yd. (46 m) sport weight #2 yarn with a long color repeat [shown in Adriafil Kimera; 100% cotton; 1.75 oz. (50 g), 148 yd. (135 m) per skein] 1 skein #014 Voltaire Fancy
- U.S. size 10$\frac{1}{2}$ (6.5 mm) knitting needles
- Framed mirror or picture frame and sheet of reflective material as insert

Gauge

Approximately 6 sts and 10 rows in St st, stretched = 4" (10 cm)

Gauge is not critical for this pattern.

Pattern Notes

- You can use whatever increase you prefer. I used a M1, but the edges won't show so you can switch it up if you like.

Special Stitches

M1 (make 1 increase): Use right needle tip to lift up the strand between the st on the right needle and the st on the left needle, place strand on left needle, knit that st through back loop.

Mirror Insert

Increase Section

Cast on 3 sts.

Row 1 (RS): K1, M1, k1, M1, k1—5 sts.

Row 2 and all remaining WS rows: Purl.

Row 3: K1, M1, k3, M1, k1—7 sts.

Row 5: K1, M1, knit across until 1 st remains, M1, k1— 9 sts.

Rep Rows 5–6 for pattern until there are 25 sts or work stretches from top left corner to bottom right corner of your mirror insert when measured on the diagonal. End with a WS row.

Decrease Section

Row 1 (RS): Ssk, knit across until 2 sts remain, k2tog— 23 sts.

Row 2 and all remaining WS rows: Purl.

Rep Rows 1–2 for pattern until 3 sts remain, ending with a WS row.

Bind off.

Finishing

Clear coat or paint your wooden frame if desired and allow to dry completely.

Stretch knitted fabric over reflective insert and place insert into outer frame.

Secure fabric edges with glue or by using leftover yarn to sew them to each other across back of insert.

Lined Basket

A soft, plush liner in an inexpensive basket adds bathroom storage that is both attractive and functional. Use the basket to store cosmetics, extra washcloths or soaps, or some reading material! When the liner gets dusty or catches a spill, just untie it and toss it in the wash.

Tip
Don't worry if the dimensions of your basket are not the same as mine! You may need to add or subtract a few stitches here or there to make it work, but the general idea remains the same.

Materials

- Approximately 80 yd. (73 m) super bulky #6 chenille yarn, in two colors [shown in Bernat Baby Blanket; 100% polyester; 10.5 oz. (300 g), 258 yd. (236 m) per skein]
  1 skein #04008 Vanilla (MC)
  1 skein #04223 Lemon Lime (CC)
- U.S. size 11 (8 mm) knitting needles, or size needed to obtain gauge
- Rectangular basket, 9" x 12" x 5" (23 x 30.5 x 12.5 cm)
- Tapestry needle
- Optional: Small amount of Velcro. If you want to secure the inside corners, stitch a small amount of the loop side of the Velcro on each corner of the liner and glue a small amount of the hook side of the Velcro into the corners of the basket.

Gauge

7.5 sts and 12 rows in St st = 4" (10 cm)

Liner

With MC, cast on 23 sts.

Knit 2 rows.

Eyelet row (RS): K1, *yo, k2tog. Rep from * across.

Knit in garter st until work measures 7" (18 cm) or the height of your basket plus 2" (5 cm), ending with a RS row.

Next two rows: With CC, knit.

With CC, continue on in St st for 8" (20.5 cm) or the interior width of your basket, ending with a RS row.

Next two rows: With CC, knit.

With MC, knit in garter st until work measures 5" (12.5 cm) or the height of your basket, ending with a WS row.

Rep Eyelet row.

Knit two more rows. Bind off.

Short Sides

With MC and RS facing, pick up 11 sts on short side of St st/CC section.

With MC, knit in garter st until work measures 5" (12.5 cm) or the height of your basket, ending with a WS row.

Rep Eyelet row.

Knit 2 more rows. Bind off.

Rep for other short side.

Finishing

With RS facing each other, sew up all 4 corner seams.

Weave in ends.

Cut a long strand of CC and weave it in and out of eyelet rows. Tie into a bow.

Flower Garden

Rose and green, violet and peach—these are the colors found in a summer garden! The projects in this section have a lacy, open look and will be beautiful in a floral, feminine bathroom with a vintage feel. Think shabby chic all grown up!

Lacy Pedicure Socks

Put these on after your soak and before your polish to keep your feet covered, clean, and dry while waiting for your polish to set. Never ruin your polish because of cold feet again!

Tip These are done in a soft cotton blend yarn for inside or spring/summer use, but you could also make a pair in a wool or wool blend for those winter days when you just *have* to leave the salon before you can risk putting on socks and shoes.

Finished Size

Approximately $8^1/_4$ " (21 cm) in circumference at both ankle and foot, 7" (18 cm) tall at center back, and 7" (18 cm) from center back to toe, all measured unblocked with the sock lying flat. The stitch pattern is very stretchy and the foot length doesn't matter because there's no toe, so sizing is not critical for this pattern.

Materials

* Approximately 150 yd. (137 m) sport weight #2 yarn [shown in Premier Yarns Cotton Fair Multi; 52% cotton, 48% acrylic; 3.5 oz. (100 g), 317 yd. (290 m) per skein] 1 skein #3203 Circus
* U.S. size 3 (3.25 mm) double-pointed needles, or size needed to obtain gauge
* Tapestry needle

Gauge

23 sts and 33 rows in St st in the round = 4" (10 cm)

Special Stitches

Sk2p: Sl 1, k2tog, pass slipped st over knit st—a double decrease.

Socks

Cast on 48 sts. Divide on DPNs with 15 sts on the first needle, 16 on the second needle, and 17 on the third needle. Join to work in the round, being careful not to twist sts. Place marker for beg of rnd.

Work 12 rnds k1, p1 ribbing.

Rnds 1–2: P2, k5, (p3, k5) 5 times, p1.

Rnd 3: P2, yo, k1, sk2p, k1, yo, (p3, yo, k1, sk2p, k1, yo) 5 times, p1.

Rnd 4: Rep Rnd 2.

Rnd 5: P2, k1, yo, sk2p, yo, k1, (p3, k1, yo, sk2p, yo, k1) 5 times, p1.

Rnds 6–8: Rep Rnd 2.

Rep Rnds 3–8 twice, then Rnds 3–6 once more.

Lacy Pedicure Socks

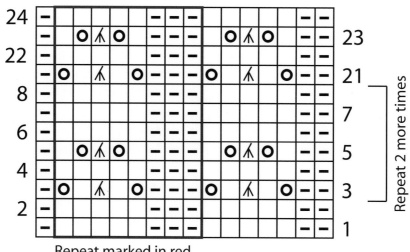

Repeat marked in red

Lacy Pedicure Socks - Gusset Needle 2

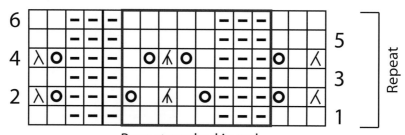

Repeat marked in red

Key

☐	k
−	p
O	yo
⋀	sk2p
⋀	k2tog
⋋	ssk

Heel Flap

Row 1 (RS): K12 sts, turn.

Row 2 (WS): Sl 1, p23, set aside remaining stitches to be worked later.

Row 3: Sl 1, *k1, sl 1. Rep from * to end.

Row 4: Sl 1, p23.

Rep Rows 3–4 for pattern until 24 rows total have been completed, ending with a WS row.

Turn Heel

Row 1 (RS): Sl 1, k14, k2tog, k1, turn—17 sts.

Row 2 (WS): Sl 1, p3, p2tog, p1, turn—6 sts.

Row 3: Sl 1, k4, k2tog, k1, turn—7 sts.

Row 4: Sl 1, p5, p2tog, p1, turn—8 sts.

Row 5: Sl 1, k6, k2tog, k1, turn—9 sts.

Row 6: Sl 1, p7, p2tog, p1, turn—10 sts.

Row 7: Sl 1, k8, k2tog, k1, turn—11 sts.

Row 8: Sl 1, p9, p2tog, p1, turn—12 sts.

Row 9: Sl 1, k10, k2tog, k1, turn—13 sts.

Row 10: Sl 1, p11, p2tog, p1, turn—14 sts

Gusset

Rnd 1: Needle 1—knit across all heel sts, pick up 12 sts down side of heel flap (1 in each sl st); needle 2—across instep work k3, (p3, k5) twice, p3, k2; needle 3—pick up 12 sts up other side of heel flap, k7 off heel flap needle for new start of rnd—19 sts on needle 1, 24 instep sts on needle 2, 19 sts on needle 3—62 sts total.

Row 2: Needle 1—knit until 3 sts remain, k2tog, k1; needle 2—k2tog, k1, yo, (p3, yo, k1, sk2p, k1, yo) twice, p3, yo, ssk; needle 3—k1, ssk, knit to end—60 sts.

Row 3: Needle 1—work even; needle 2—k3, (p3, k5) twice, p3, k2; needle 3—work even.

Row 4: Needle 1—knit until 3 sts remain, k2tog, k1; needle 2—k2tog, k1, yo, (p3, k1, yo, sk2p, yo, k1) twice, p3, yo, ssk; needle 3—k1, ssk, knit to end—58 sts.

Continue in pattern as established, maintaining lace pattern on needle 2 and decreasing 2 sts every other round until 48 sts remain.

Continue in pattern as established, maintaining lace pattern on needle 2 and working even on needles 1 and 3 until work measures 4½" (11.5 cm) from end of heel turn, ending with a row containing a sk2p.

Work in k1, p1 ribbing for 12 rows.

Bind off in ribbing.

Weave in ends.

Pink Lace Bathmat

The aim of this mat is to be pretty, not necessarily absorbent! Use it in front of your vanity or pedestal sink for a feminine touch.

Tip

Use puff paint from the fabric paint section of the craft store and put lots of dots on the wrong side of the fabric to create your own non-slip surface that won't show through the lacier parts of the stitch pattern.

Finished Size

20" x 28" (51 x 71 cm), after blocking

Materials

- Approximately 350 yd. (320 m) bulky weight #5 yarn [shown in Berroco Comfort Chunky; 50% super fine nylon, 50% super fine acrylic; 3.5 oz. (100 g), 150 yd. (137 m) per skein]
  3 skeins #5723 Rosebud
- U.S. size 9 (5.5 mm) knitting needles
- Tapestry needle

Gauge

11 sts x 18 rows in pattern st, after blocking = 4" (10 cm)
Gauge is not critical for this pattern.

Rug

Cast on 58 sts.

Knit 10 rows for garter st border.

Row 1 (WS): K5, *p2, yo, p2tog. Rep from * across until 5 sts remain, k5.

Row 2 (RS): K7, yo, ssk, *k2, yo, ssk. Rep from * across until 5 sts remain, k5.

Rep Rows 1–2 for pattern until work measures 26$\frac{1}{2}$" (67.5 cm) or 1$\frac{1}{2}$" (4 cm) less than desired length, ending with a Row 1.

Knit 10 rows for border.

Bind off.

Weave in ends.

Tray Liner

Here's another knit-accented home décor item that takes almost no time to make, but will add a unique look to any bathroom. A glass liner keeps the knitted piece clean and looking terrific forever.

Tip

This tray was found in the unpainted wood section of the local chain craft store. A quick coat of white paint was all it took to provide a high-contrast frame for the lace stitch.

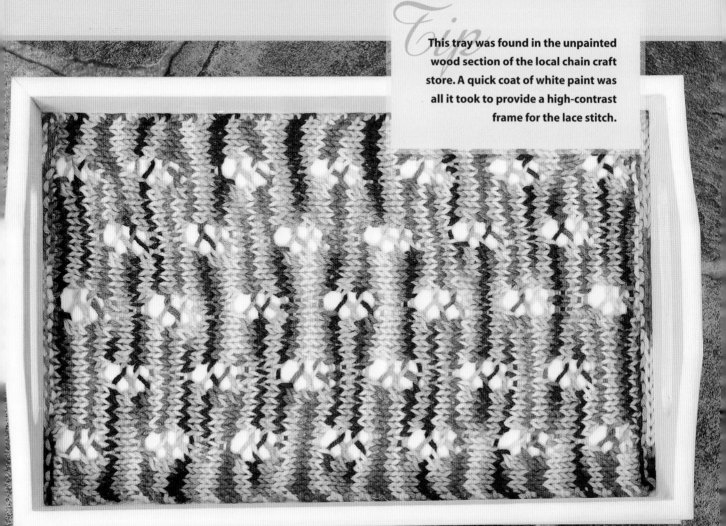

Finished Size

Approximately $7^{1}/_{4}$" x $11^{1}/_{4}$" (18.5 x 28.5 cm)

*Adjust the pattern by adding or subtracting multiples of 10
sts, and block as needed to fit your tray.*

Materials

- Approximately 40 yd. (36.5 m) DK weight #3 yarn
  [shown in Universal Yarns Bamboo Pop; 50% cotton,
  50% bamboo; 3.5 oz. (100 g), 292 yd. (267 m) per ball]
  1 ball #207 On Parade
- U.S. size 5 (3.75 mm) knitting needles, or size needed
  to obtain gauge
  Unfinished wood tray, exterior measurements $7^{1}/_{2}$" x
  $11^{1}/_{2}$" (19 x 29cm)
- Clear glass cut to fit interior measurements of tray. I
  used a recycled window pane and had it cut at the
  local hardware store.
- Fabric glue or hot glue gun and sticks

Gauge

18 sts x 30 rows in pattern st, after blocking = 4" (10 cm)

Tray Liner

Cast on 30 sts with long-tail cast-on.

Row 1 (RS): Knit.

Row 2 (WS): K1, p28, k1.

Rows 3, 5, and 7: K5, yo, k2tog, (k8, yo, k2tog) twice, k3.

Rows 4, 6, and 8: K1, p4, yo, p2tog, (p8, yo, p2tog) twice,
p2, k1.

Rows 9, 11, and 13: K10, yo, k2tog, k8, yo, k2tog, k8.

Rows 10, 12, and 14: K1, p9, yo, p2tog, p8, yo, p2tog, p7, k1.

Rep Rows 3–14 five more times, then Rows 3–8 once
   more.

Rep Row 1.

Knit 2 rows.

Bind off knitwise.

Finishing

Block to interior measurements of tray.

With fabric glue or hot glue, run a thin line of glue
   around inside edge of tray.

Press knitted fabric into place.

Lay glass on top of knitted fabric.

Tray Liner

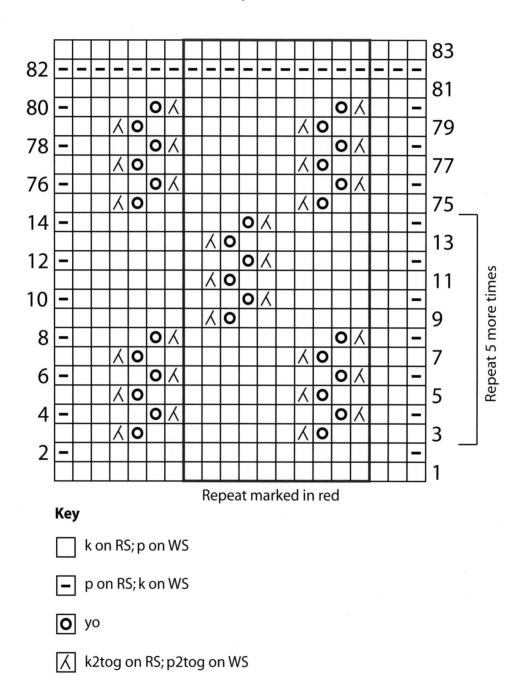

Repeat marked in red

Key

☐ k on RS; p on WS

▬ p on RS; k on WS

▣ yo

⋀ k2tog on RS; p2tog on WS

Shaped Washcloths

Simple shapes in contrasting colors make a lovely set of washcloths for any style of bathroom. All three—the triangle, circle, and square—are worked center-out, and can be started on either DPNs or with the magic loop technique.

Tip

These are great projects on which to practice shaping! You can also try stitches other than stockinette stitch—try garter stitch or seed stitch for a different look. You can make the washcloths larger or smaller by simply adding or subtracting rows.

Finished Sizes

Triangle: 8" (20.5 cm) tall x 8" (20.5 cm) wide at widest
    point
Circle: 8" (20.5 cm) diameter
Square: 8" x 8" (20.5 x 20.5 cm)

Materials

- Each washcloth takes approximately 40 yd. (27 m)
  worsted weight #4 yarn [shown in Knit Picks Dishie;
  100% cotton; 3.5 oz. (100 g), 190 yd. (174 m) per skein]
  1 skein #25784 Mulberry (Triangle)
  1 skein #25411 Conch (Circle)
  1 skein #25790 Begonia (Square)
- U.S. size 5 (3.75 mm) double-pointed needles and 16"
  (40 cm) circular needle, or size needed to obtain gauge
- Stitch marker
- Tapestry needle

Gauge

16 sts and 24 rows in St st = 4" (10 cm)

Triangle

Cast on 9 sts. Join to work in the round and place marker
    to denote beg of rnd.

Rnd 1: (Yo, k1, yo, k2) 3 times—15 sts.

Rnd 2: Knit.

Rnd 3: (K1, yo, k1, yo, k3) 3 times—21 sts.

Rnd 4 and all remaining even-numbered rows: Knit.

Rnd 5: (K2, yo, k1, yo, k4) 3 times—27 sts.

Rnd 7: (K3, yo, k1, yo, k5) 3 times—33 sts.

Continue in pattern as established, increasing 6 sts every
    other row by working yarn overs before and after each
    column of a singular St st until work measures $7^3/_4$"
    (19.5 cm) when measured along one vertical column.
    Change to circular needle when there are too many
    stitches to fit comfortably on the DPNs.

Next rnd: Purl.

Bind off knitwise.

Weave in ends using cast-on tail to tighten up the central
    cast-on.

Circle

Cast on 4 sts. Join to work in the round and place marker to denote beg of rnd.

Rnd 1: (Yo, k1) 4 times—8 sts.

Rnd 2: (Yo, k1) 8 times—16 sts.

Rnd 3 and remaining odd-numbered rnds: Knit.

Rnd 4: (Yo, k2) 8 times—24 sts.

Row 6: (Yo, k3) 8 times—32 sts.

Continue working in pattern as established, with 1 more st between yarn overs on every other row, until work measures 7³/₄" (19.5 cm) in diameter. Change to circular needle when there are too many stitches to fit comfortably on the DPNs.

Next rnd: Purl.

Bind-off knitwise.

Weave in ends.

Square

Cast on 4 sts. Join to work in the round and place marker to denote beg of rnd.

Rnd 1: Kfb 4 times—8 sts.

Rnd 2: (Yo, k1) 8 times—16 sts.

Rnd 3 and remaining odd-numbered rnds: Knit.

Rnd 4: K1, (yo, k1, yo, k3) 3 times, yo, k1, yo, k2—24 sts.

Rnd 6: K2, (yo, k1, yo, k5) 3 times, yo, k1, yo, k3—32 sts.

Rnd 8: K3, (yo, k1, yo, k7) 3 times, yo, k1, yo, k4—40 sts.

Continue in pattern as established, working 1 more st before the first yarn over at beg of rnd and 2 more sts between yarn overs in pattern st, until work measures 7³/₄" (19.5 cm) along one side. Change to circular needle when there are too many stitches to fit comfortably on the DPNs.

Next rnd: Purl.

Bind-off knitwise.

Weave in ends.

Oceantide

Nothing is as calming as the sea on a sunny day. Pamper yourself with beautiful bathroom accessories in shades of blue and green with bright white and sunny yellow accents. Rich colors offer a lush feel to an upscale bathroom, and the textures of the knitted fabrics offer exfoliating properties as well as visual interest.

Cabled Towels

A lot of style for a small amount of knitting! These cute, cabled trims fit neatly into the flat, terry-cloth-less band found on many bath and hand towels. I used a long repeat colorway to get some colorful punch, but since the stitch is textured you could also get some visual interest via a contrasting or coordinating color.

Tip Towels from different towel manufacturers have different sized bands. Use either the wide trim noted for the bath towel or the narrow trim noted for the hand towel—whichever fits your particular band!

Finished Size

Entire bath towel is 51" x 27" (129.5 x 68.5 cm); trim is
1¹/₂" x 27" (4 x 68.5 cm)

Entire hand towel is 26" x 17" (66 x 43 cm); trim is 1" x 17"
(2.5 x 43 cm)

Materials

* Approximately 15–20 yd. (14–18 m) for either size trim
  of DK weight #3 yarn [shown in Adriafil Kimera; 100%
  cotton; 1.7 oz. (50 g), 148 yd. (135 m) per skein]
  1 skein #16 Proust Fancy
* U.S. size 3 (3.25 mm) knitting needles
* Cable needle
* Tapestry needle
* Straight pins

Gauge

Gauge is not critical for this pattern.

Pattern Notes

* While gauge is not critical for this pattern, check your
  width to make sure it will fill in your towel band. Adjust
  width if needed by adding or subtracting sts on either
  side of the cable.
* Slip first st of every row.

Special Stiches

RC (right cross): Place 3 sts on cable needle and hold
behind work, knit 3 sts from left-hand needle, knit 3 sts
from cable needle.

Bath Towel Trim

Cast on 12 sts.

Row 1 and all remaining WS rows: Sl 1, k2, p6, k3.

Rows 2 and 4 (RS): Sl 1, p2, k6, p3.

Row 6: Sl 1, p2, RC, p3.

Row 8: Rep Row 2.

Rep Rows 1–8 for pattern until work measures 27"
(68.5 cm) or desired length, ending with a Row 4.
Bind off.

Hand Towel Trim

Cast on 8 sts.

Row 1 and all remaining WS rows: Sl 1, p7.

Rows 2 and 4 (RS): Sl 1, k6, p1.

Row 6: Sl 1, RC, p1.

Row 8: Rep Row 2.

Rep Rows 1–8 for pattern until work measures 17"
(43 cm) or desired length, ending with a Row 4.
Bind off.

Finishing for Both Trims

Pin trim into place on RS of towel using straight pins.

With strand of yarn and tapestry needle, sew trim into
place on towel using whipstitch at each short end and
backstitch along each long side edge.

Weave in all ends.

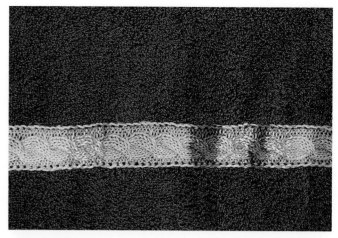

Bath towel trim

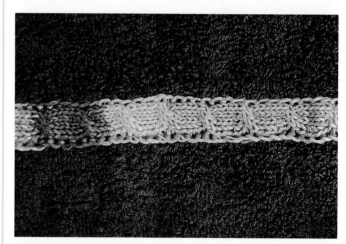

Hand towel trim

Finishing both trims, wrong side

Chevron Washcloth

Cleverly placed increases and decreases give this washcloth a chevron shape even though you're knitting straight across!

Tip

Because the side borders change color along with the stripes, there's no need for bobbins for this pattern.

Finished Size

7^1/$_2$" (19 cm) square

Materials

- 65 yd. (59.5 m) worsted weight #4 yarn [shown in Lion Brand Yarns Kitchen Cotton; 100% cotton; 2 oz. (57 g), 99 yd. (90 m) per skein]
  1 skein #831-106 Blueberry (A)
  1 skein #831-130 Snap Pea (B)
- U.S. size 6 (4 mm) knitting needles, or size needed to obtain gauge
- Tapestry needle

Gauge

19 sts x 23 rows in pattern st, after blocking = 4" (10 cm)

Special Stitches

Sk2p: Sl 1, k2tog, pass slipped st over knit st—a double decrease.

Washcloth

First Border

With A, cast on 33 sts with long-tail cast-on. Knit 5 more rows.

Body

Row 1 (WS): K3, p27, k3.
Rows 2 – 8 (RS): With B, k3, yo, k5, sk2p, k5, yo, k1, yo, k5, sk2p, k5, yo, k3.
Row 9: With A, rep Row 2.
Rows 10 –11: With A, knit.
Rep Rows 2–11 twice.

Second Border

With A, knit 4 more rows.
Bind off.
Weave in ends.

Textured Bath Mitt

Bath mitts are terrific for the tub, whether you are washing yourself or someone else! Tightly knit for a lot of texture, you won't be dropping this a dozen times like you might with a washcloth.

Tip

Embroider on some eyes and a smiley face for a bathtub monster for your favorite little one.

Finished Size

9¹/₂" (24 cm) tall x 6" (15cm) wide at widest point, laid
flat, hem unrolled

Materials

- 125 yd. (114 m) DK weight #3 yarn [shown in Plymouth
  Cleo DK Cotton; 100% cotton; 1.7 oz. (50 g), 125 yd.
  (114 m) per skein]
  1 skein #0175 Cleo Shamrock
- U.S. size 3 (3.25 mm) double-pointed needles, or size
  needed to obtain gauge
- 3 stitch markers, 1 different for start of round
- Small stitch holder
- Tapestry needle

Gauge

16 sts and 18 rows in pattern st, after blocking = 4"
(10 cm)

Bath Mitt

Cuff

Cast on 48 sts onto DPNs. Join for knitting in the round,
being careful not to twist sts. Place marker for beg
of rnd.

Knit 12 rnds for rolled St st edging.

BEGIN PATTERN STITCH

Rnds 1 and 3: *P4, k2. Rep from * around.

Rnd 2 and remaining even-numbered rnds: Knit.

Rnds 5 and 7: P1, k2, *p4, k2. Rep from * around until
3 sts remain, p3.

Rep Rnds 1–8 once more.

Start Thumb

Rnd 1: (P4, k2) 4 times, place marker, M1, place marker, (p4, k2) 4 times—49 sts.

Rnd 2 and remaining even-numbered rnds: Knit.

Rnd 3: (P4, k2) 4 times, sl marker, M1, knit to next marker, M1, sl marker, (p4, k2) 4 times—51 sts.

Rnds 5 and 7: P1, k2, (p4, k2) 3 times, p3, sl marker, M1, knit to next marker, M1, sl marker, p1, k2, (p4, k2) 3 times, p3—53 sts after Rnd 5; 55 sts after Rnd 7.

Rnd 9: Rep Rnd 3—57 sts.

Rnds 11–20: Rep Rnds 3–10, then Rnds 3–4. There will be 19 sts between markers.

Palm

Rnd 1: (P4, k2) 4 times, place next 19 sts on stitch holder and set aside for later, remove markers, (p4, k2) 4 times—48 sts.

Rep Rnds 2–8 of Cuff, then Rnds 1–8 of Cuff.

Decrease Section

Rnd 1: (K1, k2tog, p1, k2, (p4, k2) twice, p3, ssk, k1) twice—44 sts.

Rnd 3: (K1, k2tog, k2, (p4, k2) twice, p2, ssk, k1) twice—40 sts.

Rnd 5: (K1, k2tog, p2, k2, p4, k2, p4, ssk, k1) twice—36 sts.

Rnd 7: (K1, k2tog, p1, k2, p4, k2, p3, ssk, k1) twice—32 sts.

Rnd 9: (K1, k2tog, p3, k2, p4, k1, ssk, k1) twice—28 sts.

Rnd 11: (K1, k2tog, p2, k2, p4, ssk, k1) twice—24 sts.

Rnd 13: (K1, k2tog, p4, k2, ssk, k1) twice—20 sts.

Rnd 15: (K1, k2tog, p3, k1, ssk, k1) twice—16 sts.

Rnd 17: (K1, k2tog, p2, ssk, k1) twice—12 sts.

Fold tops flat and graft first 6 sts to last 6 sts using either Kitchener stitch or three-needle bind-off.

Thumb

Place 19 sts on DPNs and set up for knitting in the round, pick up 2 more sts in gap between first and last st—21 sts.

Knit 15 rows or $3/8$" (1 cm) less than desired thumb height.

Decrease Section

Rnd 1: *K1, k2tog. Rep from * around—14 sts.

Rnd 2: Knit.

Rnd 3: K2tog 7 times—7 sts.

Rnd 4: Knit.

Cut yarn, leaving a 6"–8" (15–20.5 cm) tail. Thread tail into tapestry needle and put needle through all 7 live sts. Pull tightly to finish thumb, end off, and weave in end.

Finishing

Weave in remaining ends.

Slip Stitch Trio of Washcloths

Slip stitch patterns are terrific for washcloths. They add some depth to the fabric and give you terrific visual punch while ensuring that you still only have to knit the pattern stitch with one color at a time. Try all three of these slip stitch patterns!

Tip

Use a bobbin or second ball of yarn for the second garter stitch border to cut down on the height of the floats seen on the wrong side of the work when changing colors.

Finished Size

8" (20.5 cm) square

Materials

- 215 yd. (197 m) worsted weight #4 yarn [shown in Lily Sugar 'n Cream; 100% cotton; 2.5 oz. (71 g), 120 yd. (110 m) per skein (A); and Lily Sugar 'n Cream Ombre;100% cotton; 2 oz. (57 g), 95 yd. (87 m) per skein (B)]
  1 skein #10200100001 White (A)
  1 skein #102002027 Swimming Pool (B)
- U.S. size 6 (4 mm) knitting needles, or size needed to obtain gauge
- Tapestry needle

Gauge

16 sts and 26 rows in Honeycomb pattern, after blocking = 4" (10 cm)

Gauge is not critical for these patterns but washcloths do best with a firm fabric.

Pattern Notes

- Slip all stitches purlwise.
- When slipping stitches, working yarn is always carried on the wrong side of the work.

Honeycomb

With A, cast on 33 sts.

Knit 6 rows for garter stitch border.

Row 1 (WS): K3, p27, k3.

Row 2 (RS): With A k3, with B k4, sl 1 wyib, (k5, sl 1 wyib) 3 times, k4, with A k3.

Row 3: With A k3, with B p4, sl 1 wyib, (p5, sl 1 wyib) 3 times, p4, with A k3.

Rows 4 and 5: Rep Rows 2–3.

Row 6: With A, knit across, including slipped sts.

Row 7: With A, k3, p27, k3.

Row 8: With A k3, with B k1, sl 1 wyib, (k5, sl 1 wyib) 4 times, k1, with A k3.

Row 9: With A k3, with B p1, sl 1 wyib, (p5, sl 1 wyib) 4 times, p1, with A k3.

Rows 10 and 11: Rep Rows 8 and 9.

Rows 12 and 13: Rep Rows 6 and 7.

Rep Rows 2–13 twice, then Rows 2–7 once more.

Knit 6 rows for garter stitch border.

Bind off.

Weave in ends.

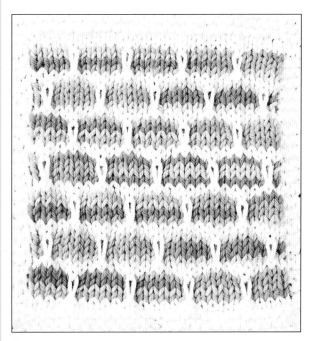

Honeycomb

Honeycomb Washcloth

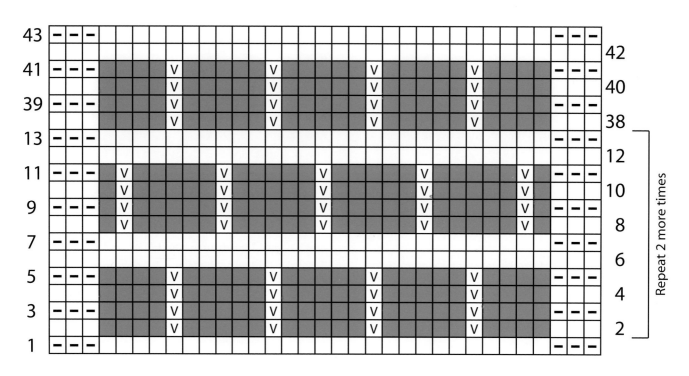

Stitch Key

☐ k on RS; p on WS

⊟ p on RS; k on WS

Ⅴ sl purlwise with
   yarn at WS of work

Color Key

☐ A

▨ B

Textured Dots

With A, cast on 33 sts.

Knit 6 rows for garter stitch border.

Row 1 (WS): K3, p27, k3.

Row 2 (RS): With A k3, with B k1, (sl 1 wyib, k1) 13 times, with A k3.

Row 3: Rep Row 2.

Row 4: With A, knit across, including slipped stitches.

Row 5: With A, k3, p27, k3.

Row 6: With A, knit.

Row 7: Rep Row 5.

Rep Rows 2–7 six times, then Rows 2–5 once more.

Knit 6 rows for garter stitch border.

Bind off.

Weave in ends.

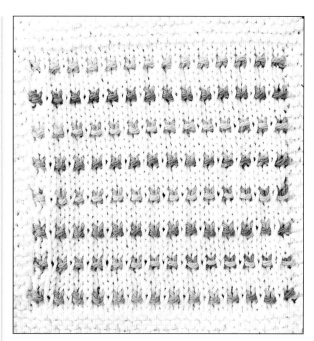

Textured Dots

Medallions

With A, cast on 35 sts.

Knit 6 rows for garter stitch border.

Row 1 (WS): With A, k3, p29, k3.

Row 2 (RS): With A k3, with B k1, (sl 3 wyib, with B k3) 4 times, sl 3 wyib, with B k1, with A k3.

Row 3: With A k3, with B p2, (sl 1 wyif, with B p5) 4 times, sl 1 wyif, with B p2, with A k3.

Row 4: With A k3, with B k29, with A k3.

Row 5: With A k3, with B k4, (p3, k3) 3 times, p3, k4, with A k3.

Row 6: With A k7, (sl 3 wyib, with A k3) 3 times, sl 3 wyib, with A k7.

Row 7: With A k3, p5, (sl 1 wyif, with A p5) 4 times, with A k3.

Row 8: With A, knit across.

Row 9: With A, k4, (p3, k3) 4 times, p3, k4.

Rep Rows 2–9 five times more.

With A, knit 6 rows for second border.

Bind off.

Weave in ends.

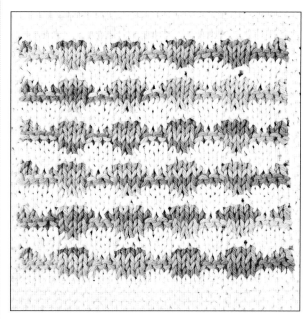

Medallions

Sunny Days

Prepare for the day in a bright bathroom accented with the golds, yellows, and oranges of a bright, sunny day. Nothing will perk up your mood more quickly!

Edged Towels

Nothing updates a set of towels more quickly than a snazzy, sewn-on edging! This one has a lozenge of stockinette stitch inserted into a garter stitch band and a scalloped edge. Use a multicolored yarn as I did here or go with a solid in a coordinating or contrasting color.

Tip

The edging for the bath towel and the hand towel is the same; the only thing that changes is the number of repeats. When there are two numbers, the first is for the hand towel and the one in parentheses is for the bath towel.

Finished Size

Entire bath towel is 51" x 27" (129.5 x 68.5 cm); trim is
1.5" x 27" (4 x 68.5 cm)

Entire hand towel is 26" x 17" (66 x 43 cm); trim is 1.5" x
17" (4 x 43 cm)

Materials

- Approximately 15–20 yd. (14–18 m) for either size trim
of worsted weight #4 yarn [shown in Lily Sugar 'n
Cream Ombre; 100% cotton; 2 oz. (57 g), 95 yd. (87 m)
per skein]
1 skein #19605 Creamsicle
- U.S. size 7 (4.5 mm) knitting needles
- Tapestry needle
- Straight pins

Gauge

13 sts and 16 rows in pattern st = 4" (10 cm)

Gauge is not critical for this project.

Special Stitches

Sk2p: Sl 1, k2tog, pass slipped st over knit st—a double
decrease.

Pattern Notes

- While gauge is not critical for this pattern, check your
width to make sure it will fit your towel. Adjust width if
needed by adding or subtracting rows.

Towel Edging

Cast on 10 sts with long-tail cast-on.

Knit 2 more rows.

Lace Pattern

Row 1 (RS): K5, k2tog, yo, k1, yo, k2—11 sts.
Row 2 (WS): K3, p1, k7.
Row 3: K4, k2tog, yo, k3, yo, k2—12 sts.
Row 4: K3, p3, k6.
Row 5: K3, k2tog, yo, k5, yo, k2—13 sts.
Row 6: K3, p5, k5.
Row 7: K5, yo, ssk, k1, k2tog, yo, k2tog, k1—12 sts.
Row 8: K3, p3, k6.
Row 9: K6, yo, sk2p, yo, k2tog, k1—11 sts.
Row 10: K3, p1, k7.
Row 11: K6, k2tog, yo, k2tog, k1—10 sts.
Row 12: Knit.
Rep Rows 1–10 for pattern until work measures 17 (27)"
[43 (68.5) cm] or slightly less than the width of your
towel, ending with a Row 10.
Knit 2 more rows.
Bind off.
Weave in ends.

Lace Pattern

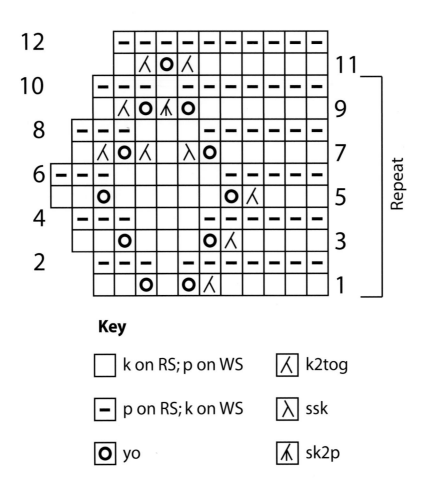

Key

	k on RS; p on WS		k2tog
	p on RS; k on WS		ssk
	yo		sk2p

Textured Linen Washcloth

Linen washcloths look terrific and wear like iron—linen is the only natural fiber that is stronger wet than dry! While it might feel a little stiff when you are stitching, the fiber will soften with use and washing.

Tip
Yarn is held double throughout. These make terrific gifts; pair with a soap or a soak for a spa theme.

Finished Size

8" (20.5 cm) square

Materials

- 130 yd. (119 m) DK weight #3 linen yarn [shown in Fibra Natura Flax; 100% linen; 1.7 oz. (50 g), 137 yd. (125 m) per skein]
  1 skein #03 Orange
- U.S. size 5 (3.75 mm) knitting needles, or size needed to obtain gauge
- Tapestry needle

Gauge

19 sts and 32 rows in pattern st = 4" (10 cm)

Washcloth

With yarn held double, cast on 30 sts.
Knit 10 rows for border.

Triangle Stitch Section

Row 1 (WS): K5, *k1, p4. Rep from * across until 5 sts remain, k5.

Row 2 and all remaining RS rows: Knit.

Row 3: K5, *k2, p3. Rep from * across until 5 sts remain, k5.

Row 5: K5, *k3, p2. Rep from * across until 5 sts remain, k5.

Row 7: K5, *k4, p1. Rep from * across until 5 sts remain, k5.

Row 9: Knit.

Rep Rows 1–10 for pattern 4 times more.

Knit 10 more rows for second border.

Bind off.

Weave in ends.

Linen Washcloth

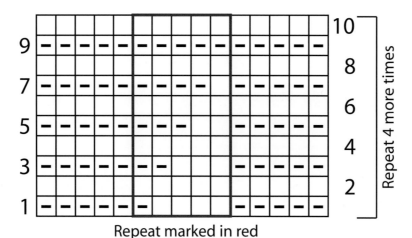

Repeat marked in red

Repeat 4 more times

Key

▢ k on RS; p on WS

⊟ p on RS; k on WS

Diagonal Washcloth

Washcloths are not only useful items, they are also great practice projects for learning new skills. This lace pattern has a strong diagonal look and is very easy to "read," making it a perfect first lace project.

Tip

The washcloth will tend to pull on the diagonal while you're knitting, but it will easily block square once the borders are on.

49

Finished Size

8" (20.5 cm) square

Materials

- Approximately 80 yd. (73 m) DK weight #3 yarn [shown in Omega Emilia; 100% cotton; 3.5 oz. (100 g), 164 yd. (150 m) per skein]
  1 skein #09 Orange Plus
- U.S. size 4 (3.5 mm) knitting needles, or size needed to obtain gauge.
- Tapestry needle

Gauge

18 sts and 32 rows in pattern st = 4" (10 cm)

Washcloth

Cast on 39 sts.
Knit 10 rows for garter st border.

Lace Pattern

Row 1 and all WS rows until second border: K5, p29, k5.
Row 2: K6, [(k2tog, yo) twice, k2] 4 times, (k2tog, yo) twice, k5.
Row 4: K5, [(k2tog, yo) twice, k2] 4 times, (k2tog, yo) twice, k6.
Row 6: K6, k2tog, yo, k2, [(k2tog, yo) twice, k2] 3 times, (k2tog, yo) twice, k7.
Row 8: K5, k2tog, yo, k2, [(k2tog, yo) twice, k2] 3 times, k8.
Row 10: K8, [(k2tog, yo) twice, k2] 4 times, k2tog, yo, k5.
Row 12: K7, [(k2tog, yo) twice, k2] 4 times, k2tog, yo, k6.
Rep Rows 1–12 for pattern until work measures 7" (18 cm), ending with a RS row.
Knit 10 rows for second garter stitch border.
Bind off.
Weave in ends.

Diagonal Washcloth

Key

☐ k on RS; p on WS

⊟ p on RS; k on WS

◙ yo

λ k2tog on RS

Storage Basket

Perfect to hold cosmetics, hair accessories, or shaving supplies, this super quick-to-stitch basket is firm enough to stand up on its own without having to add stiffeners. Made of four shades of acrylic yarn held together for a tweedy look, it's also machine washable.

Tip
This project is a terrific stash buster if you use four different colors, but you could also use four strands of the same color for a subtler look.

Finished Size

6" (15cm) tall x 10" (25.5 cm) across x 28" (71 cm) in circumference

Materials

- 600 yd. (548.5 cm) worsted weight #4 yarn in contrasting colors [shown in Lion Brand Yarn Vanna's Choice; 100% premium acrylic; 3.5 oz. (100 g), 170 yd. (156 m) per skein]
  1 skein #860-157 Radiant Yellow
  1 skein #860-100 White
  1 skein #860-123 Beige
  1 skein #860-132 Radiant Orange.
- U.S. size 11 (8 mm) double-pointed needles and 16" (40 cm) circular needle, or size needed to obtain gauge
- Stitch marker
- Tapestry needle

Gauge

8 sts and 14 rows in St st with four strands held together = 4" (10 cm)

Gauge is not critical but fabric should be stiff so the basket can remain upright with wear.

Special Stitches

Kfb (knit 1 front and back, an increase): Knit into front of st, do not push st off left needle, knit into back of same st, push off left needle.

Basket

With 4 strands held together (1 strand each of 4 colors), cast on 4 sts onto DPNs. Set up for knitting in the round, being careful not to twist. Place st marker to denote start of rnd.

Rnd 1: Kfb in each st around—8 sts.
Rnd 2 and all remaining even-numbered rnds: Knit.
Rnd 3: Rep Rnd 1—16 sts.
Rnd 5: (Kfb, k1) 8 times—24 sts.
Rnd 7: (Kfb, k2) 8 times—32 sts.
Rnd 9: (Kfb, k3) 8 times—40 sts.
Rnd 10: (Kfb, k4) 8 times—48 sts.

Rnd 12: (Kfb, k5) 8 times—56 sts.
Rnd 14: (Kfb, k6) 8 times—64 sts.

Knit each rnd until work measures 8" (20.5 cm) from central cast-on or 1" (2.5 cm) less than desired height. Change from DPNs to circular needle when work is too large to fit comfortably on the DPNs. At end of last rnd, cut yarn leaving a long tail.

Edging (Applied I-Cord)

With 4 strands held together, cast 4 sts onto one DPN. Do not turn work, slide work to right-hand side of needle.

Rnd 1: Knit 3 sts from DPN, k2tog with last st on DPN and first st on circular needle. Do not turn, slide work to right-hand side of needle.

Rnd 2: Knit 3 sts from DPN, k2tog with last st on DPN and next st on circular needle. Do not turn, slide work to right-hand side of needle.

Rep Rnd 2 for pattern until all sts have been knit off of the circular needle.

Do not bind off; cut long tail of all 4 strands of yarn and, using the tapestry needle, stitch the live sts into place to the first sts of the round. End off.

Weave in ends.

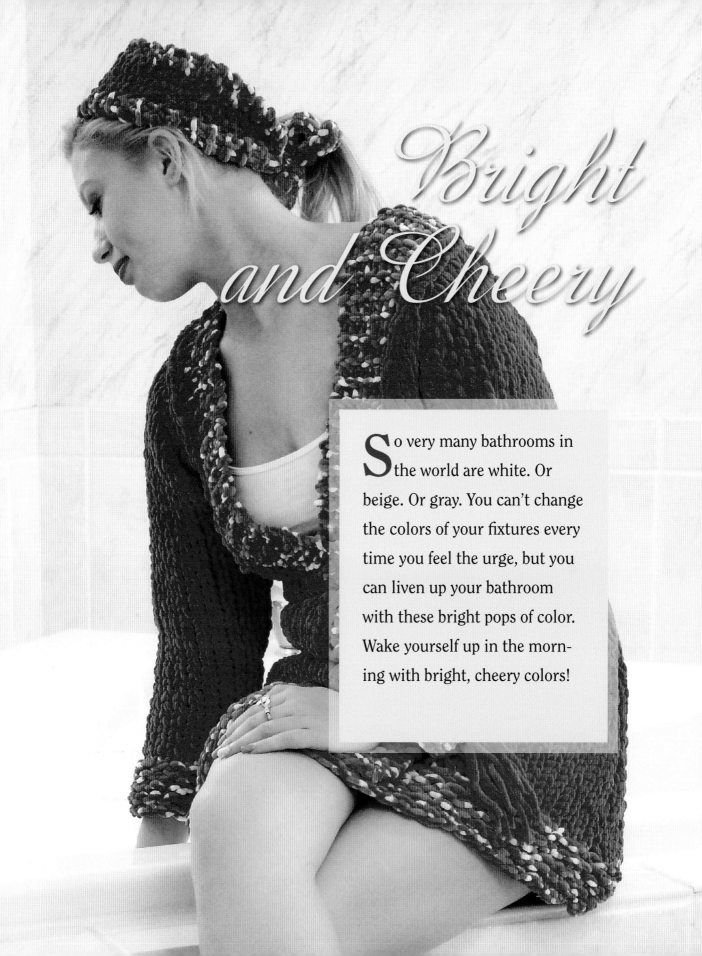

Bright and Cheery

So very many bathrooms in the world are white. Or beige. Or gray. You can't change the colors of your fixtures every time you feel the urge, but you can liven up your bathroom with these bright pops of color. Wake yourself up in the morning with bright, cheery colors!

Chenille Set

While I was told it would be crazy to knit a bathrobe, holding bulky yarn double on large knitting needles made it knit up a lot more quickly than you would expect! So plush, so thick and cozy—come on, you know you want one!

Tip **Make sure you get some puffy fabric paint or fabric with rubberized dots on it for the bottom of the slipper socks so you don't slide all over your wet floor!**

Finished Size

Bathrobe: XS (S, M, L, XL, 2X), to fit bust 34 (38, 42, 46, 50, 54)" [86.5 (96.5, 106.5, 117, 127, 137) cm] (Model shown in XS)

Socks: Cuff opening is 12" (30.5 cm) in circumference; foot is 11" (28 cm) in circumference and 9" (23 cm) long, although length is easily adjustable

Headband: 4" (10 cm) wide x 20" (51 cm) long, excluding ties

Materials

* Approximately 1300 (1560, 1820, 1950, 2340, 2600) yd. [1189 (1426, 1664, 1783, 2140, 2377) m] super bulky #6 chenille yarn [shown in Universal Yarn Bella Chenille; 100% polyester; 3.5 oz. (100 g), 131 yd. (120 m) per skein] for complete set

  8 (9, 11, 12, 14, 15) skeins #107 Ripe Berry (MC)

  2 (3, 3, 4, 4, 5) skeins #306 Sweetness (CC)

  Note: Headband only takes part of 1 skein each of MC and CC. Socks take 2 skeins MC and part of 1 skein of CC.

* U.S. size 11 (8.0 mm) knitting needles, or size needed to obtain gauge. Headband and socks require double-pointed needles; bathrobe does not.
* Tapestry needle with a very large eye
* For headband: 2 large bobbins
* For socks: large stitch marker

Gauge

6 sts and 10 rows in St st with yarn held double = 4" (10 cm)

Special Stitches

Sk2p: Sl 1, k2tog, pass slipped st over knit st—a double decrease.

Pattern Notes

* Yarn is held double throughout.

Bathrobe

Back

HEM

With 1 strand each MC and CC held together, cast on 40 (44, 46, 50, 52, 56) sts with long-tail cast-on.

Knit 9 more rows for garter st border. Break off CC.

BODY

With 2 strands MC held together, work in St st for approximately 3" (7.5 cm), beg and ending with a WS row.

Dec 1 st at beg and end of next RS row.

Continue in St st, dec at the beg and end of a RS row every 4" (10 cm) until you have 28 (32, 34, 36, 38, 42) sts.

Work even in St st until work measures approximately 26 (27, 28, 29, 30, 31)" [66 (68.5, 71, 73.5, 76, 78.5) cm] from cast-on edge, ending with a WS row.

ARMHOLE SHAPING

Continue in St st, dec 1 st at beg and end of each RS row 3 (4, 5, 5, 5, 6) times—22 (24, 24, 26, 28, 30) sts after all decreases for your size have been completed.

Work even in St st until armhole measures approximately 5 (5, 6, 6, 7, 7)" [12.5 (12.5, 15, 15, 18, 18) cm], ending with a RS row.

End off 1 strand of MC. With 1 strand each MC and CC, knit 9 rows for garter st edging; bind off knitwise.

Right Front

Note: Maintain first 5 sts (with RS facing) in garter st with 1 strand each of MC and CC.

With 1 strand each MC and CC held together, cast on 24 (25, 27, 28, 30, 31) sts.

Knit 9 more rows for garter st border.

Row 1: Knit 5, drop strand of CC, with 2 strands MC knit to end of row.

Row 2: Purl across until 5 sts remain, drop one strand MC, with 1 strand each MC and CC knit 5.

Bathrobe

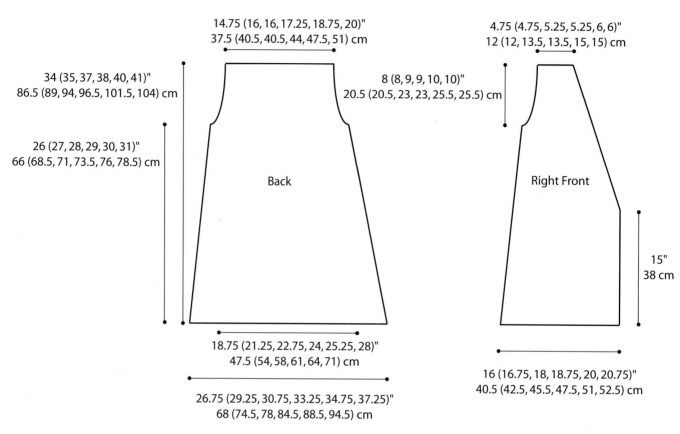

14.75 (16, 16, 17.25, 18.75, 20)"
37.5 (40.5, 40.5, 44, 47.5, 51) cm

4.75 (4.75, 5.25, 5.25, 6, 6)"
12 (12, 13.5, 13.5, 15, 15) cm

34 (35, 37, 38, 40, 41)"
86.5 (89, 94, 96.5, 101.5, 104) cm

8 (8, 9, 9, 10, 10)"
20.5 (20.5, 23, 23, 25.5, 25.5) cm

26 (27, 28, 29, 30, 31)"
66 (68.5, 71, 73.5, 76, 78.5) cm

Back

Right Front

15"
38 cm

18.75 (21.25, 22.75, 24, 25.25, 28)"
47.5 (54, 58, 61, 64, 71) cm

26.75 (29.25, 30.75, 33.25, 34.75, 37.25)"
68 (74.5, 78, 84.5, 88.5, 94.5) cm

16 (16.75, 18, 18.75, 20, 20.75)"
40.5 (42.5, 45.5, 47.5, 51, 52.5) cm

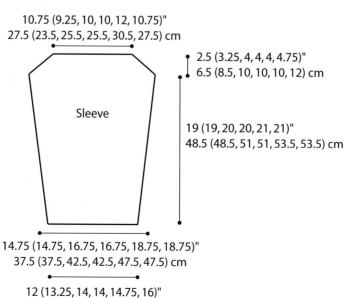

10.75 (9.25, 10, 10, 12, 10.75)"
27.5 (23.5, 25.5, 25.5, 30.5, 27.5) cm

2.5 (3.25, 4, 4, 4, 4.75)"
6.5 (8.5, 10, 10, 10, 12) cm

Sleeve

19 (19, 20, 20, 21, 21)"
48.5 (48.5, 51, 51, 53.5, 53.5) cm

14.75 (14.75, 16.75, 16.75, 18.75, 18.75)"
37.5 (37.5, 42.5, 42.5, 47.5, 47.5) cm

12 (13.25, 14, 14, 14.75, 16)"
30.5 (33.5, 35.5, 35.5, 37.5, 40.5) cm

Work as established, maintaining 5 sts in garter st with 1 strand each MC and CC and working St st with 2 strands MC, while at the same time decreasing 1 st at the end of a RS row every 4" (10 cm), until work measures 15" (38 cm) (all sizes) from cast-on edge.

Maintaining left edge decrease as established until 6 (6, 6, 7, 7, 7) decreases have been made, *at the same time* dec 1 st at the neck edge every other RS row by working a ssk after the color change until work measures 26 (27, 28, 29, 30, 31)" [66 (68.5, 71, 73.5, 76, 78.5) cm] from cast on-edge, ending with a WS row.

ARMHOLE SHAPING

Maintain neck edge shaping as established while *at the same time* dec 1 st at beg of every WS row 3 (4, 5, 5, 5, 6) times.

Continue in pattern as established until armhole measures 8 (8, 9, 9, 10, 10)" [20.5 (20.5, 23, 23, 25.5, 25.5) cm], ending neck edge decreasing when you have 7 (7, 8, 8, 9, 9) sts remaining.

Bind off.

Left Front

Work as for Right Front, reversing all shaping.

Sleeves (Make 2)

HEM

With 1 strand each MC and CC held together, cast on 18 (20, 21, 21, 22, 24) sts.

Knit 9 more rows for garter st border. Break off CC.

SLEEVE BODY

With 2 strands MC held together, work in St st, increasing 1 st at beg and end of a RS row every 3 (3, 2, 2, 2, 2)" [7.5 (7.5, 5, 5, 5, 5) cm] 2 (1, 2, 2, 3, 2) times—22 (22, 25, 25, 28, 28) sts when all increases for your size have been completed.

Work even in St st if necessary until work measures 19 (19, 20, 20, 21, 21)" [48.5 (48.5, 51, 51, 53.5, 53.5) cm] from cast-on edge, ending with a WS row.

ARMHOLE DECREASES

Continue in St st, binding off 1 st at the beg and end of each RS row 3 (4, 5, 5, 5, 6) times. Work 1 final WS row; bind off knitwise—16 (14, 15, 15, 18, 16) sts when all decreases for your size have been completed.

Finishing

Seam fronts to back at shoulders. Seam top of sleeve to body. Seam underarm and side seam of body. Cut 9 strands of yarn 72" (183 cm) long. Braid together for bathrobe belt.

Headband

Note: Wind off bobbins of 7–8 yd. (6–7 m) each of MC and CC.

First Tie

With one strand MC and one strand CC held together (not the bobbins), cast 3 sts onto DPN.

Work in I-cord for 12" (30.5 cm) or desired length of tie.

Headband

Row 1: Changing to straight or circular needles and working in rows, k1, M1, k1, M1, k1—5 sts.

Row 2: Knit.

Row 3: K1, M1, k3, M1, k1—7 sts.

Row 4: Knit.

Row 5 (WS): K2, drop CC, with 2 strands MC p3, drop MC bobbin, with 1 strand MC and CC bobbin k2.

Row 6 (RS): K2, drop CC bobbin, with 2 strands MC k3, drop MC bobbin, with 1 strand each MC and CC k2.

Rep Rows 5–6 for pattern until work measures 19" (48.5 cm) from start of rows, ending with a RS row.

Next row (WS): With 1 strand each MC and CC, knit across. End off bobbins.

Next row (RS): K1, k2tog, k1, k2tog, k1—5 sts.

Next row: K1, (k2tog) twice—3 sts.

Next row: Knit.

Second Tie

Change to DPNS and continue on in a 3-st I-cord for 12" (30.5 cm) or desired length of tie.

Bind off.

Finishing

Weave in all ends.

Slipper Socks

Cuff

With 1 strand A and 1 strand B held together, cast 18 sts
onto DPNs. Join to work in the round, being careful not
to twist sts. Place marker for beg of rnd.
Knit 10 rnds garter stitch (alternate knit rnds and purl
rnds)
End off color B.
With 2 strands A held together, knit 2 rnds.

Heel Flap

Row 1 (RS): K5, turn.
Row 2 (WS): Sl 1, p8, set aside remaining stitches to be
worked later.
Row 3: Sl 1, k8.
Rep Rows 2–3 for pattern until flap measures 2^1/$_2$"
(6.5 cm), ending with a WS row.

Turn Heel

Row 1(RS): Sl 1, k5, k2tog, k1, turn—8 sts.
Row 2(WS): Sl 1, p4, p2tog, p1, turn—7 sts.
Row 3: Sl 1, k4, k2tog, turn—6 sts.
Row 4: Sl 1, p3, p2tog, turn—5 sts.

Gusset

Rnd 1: Knit across all heel sts, pick up and knit 4 sts down
side of heel flap, with second DPN knit across 9 instep
sts, with third DPN pick up and knit 4 sts up side of
heel flap, knit 2 sts from first needle and mark new
start of rnd.
There are 7 sts on the first needle, 9 on the second, and 6
on the third—22 sts.
Rnds 2 and 4: Knit until 2 sts remain on first needle,
k2tog, knit across second needle, on third needle ssk,
knit to end—20 sts after Rnd 2; 18 after Rnd 4 with 5
on first needle, 9 on second needle, and 4 on third
needle.

Rnds 3 and 5: Knit.
Work even in St st (knit every rnd) until work measures 7"
(18 cm) from bottom of heel flap or 2" (5 cm) less than
your desired foot length.

Toe

Rnd 1: On first needle, k2, k2tog, k1; on second needle,
k1, ssk, k3, k2tog, k1; on third needle, k1, ssk, k1—14 sts.
Rnds 2, 4, and 6: Knit.
Rnd 3: On first needle, k1, k2tog, k1; on second needle, k1,
ssk, k1, k2tog, k1; on third needle, k1, ssk—10 sts.
Rnd 5: On first needle, k1, k2tog; on second needle, k1,
sk2p, k1; on third needle, k1, sl 1, psso first st of first
needle—6 sts.

Finishing

Graft toe with Kitchener st.
Weave in all ends.

Faux Cable Washcloth

Just because it's twisty doesn't mean it's cabled! A little bit of lace gives this washcloth a lot of depth, but it's still super simple to make.

Tip

This stitch pattern is made with properly placed yarn overs and decreases and doesn't require a cable needle at all.

Finished Size

8" (20.5 cm) square

Materials

- 65 yd. (59.5 cm) worsted weight #4 yarn [shown in Premier Home Cotton Solids; 85% cotton, 15% polyester; 2.82 oz. (80 g), 140 yd. (128 m) per skein] 1 skein #3809 Fuchsia
- U.S. size 6 (4 mm) knitting needles, or size needed to obtain gauge
- Tapestry needle

Gauge

17 sts and 22 rows in pattern st, after blocking = 4" (10 cm)

Washcloth

First Border

Cast on 37 sts with long-tail cast-on.

Knit 5 more rows.

Body

Row 1 and all WS rows until border: K4, p9, (k1, p9) twice, k4.

Row 2 (RS): K3, p1, (yo, k3, ssk, k4, p1) 3 times, k3.

Row 4: K3, p1, (k1, yo, k3, ssk, k3, p1) 3 times, k3.

Row 6: K3, p1, (k2, yo, k3, ssk, k2, p1) 3 times, k3.

Row 8: K3, p1, (k3, yo, k3, ssk, k1, p1) 3 times, k3.

Row 10: K3, p1, (k4, yo, k3, ssk, p1) 3 times, k3.

Row 12: K3, p1, (k9, p1) 3 times, k3.

Rep Rows 1–12 three more times, then Row 1 once more.

Second Border

Knit 6 more rows.

Bind off.

Weave in ends.

Faux Cable Washcloth

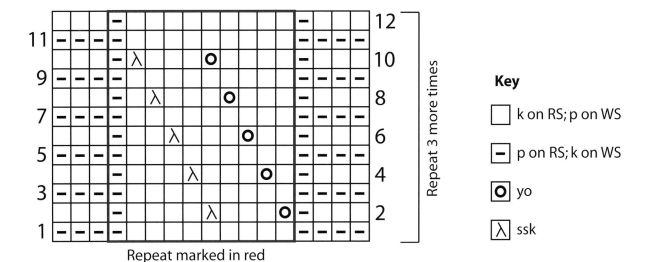

Repeat marked in red

Repeat 3 more times

Key

- [ ] k on RS; p on WS
- [−] p on RS; k on WS
- [O] yo
- [λ] ssk

Acorn Pattern Washcloth

Alternating panels of garter stitch and stockinette stitch set off by symmetrically placed yarn overs give you an interesting pattern that looks like staggered rows of acorns!

Tip

Textured blocks and lacy yarn overs—this washcloth has a little bit of everything. It's a very intuitive pattern to read, once you get started, and is not as challenging as it looks!

Finished Size

7.5" (19 cm) square

Materials

- 65 yd. (59.5 cm) worsted weight #4 yarn [shown in Premier Home Cotton Solids; 85% cotton, 15% polyester; 2.82 oz. (80 g), 140 yd. (128 m) per skein] 1 skein #3809 Fuchsia
- U.S. size 6 (4 mm) knitting needles, or size needed to obtain gauge
- Tapestry needle

Gauge

15 sts x 26 rows in pattern st, after blocking = 4" (10 cm)

Special Stitches

Sk2p: Sl 1, k2tog, pass slipped st over knit st—a double decrease.

Washcloth

First Border

Cast on 33 sts with long-tail cast-on.

Knit 5 more rows.

Body

Rows 1, 3, and 5 (WS): K6, p3, (k3, p3) 3 times, k6.
Rows 2 and 4 (RS): Knit.
Row 6: K6, yo, sk2p, yo, (k3, yo, sk2p, yo) 3 times, k6.
Rows 7, 9, and 11: K3, (p3, k3) 5 times.
Rows 8 and 10: Knit.
Row 12: K3, yo, sk2p, yo, (k3, yo, sk2p, yo) 4 times, k3.
Rep Rows 1–12 twice, then Rows 1–5 once more.

Second Border

Knit 6 more rows.
Bind off.
Weave in ends.

Acorn Washcloth

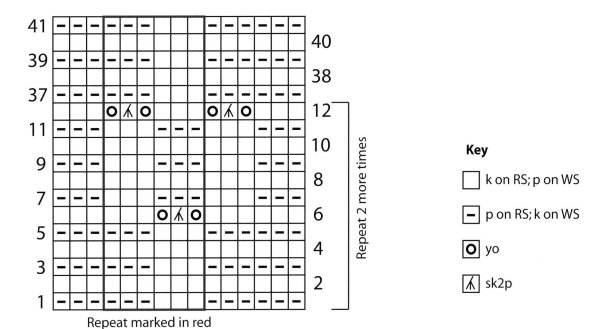

Repeat marked in red

Key

k on RS; p on WS

− p on RS; k on WS

O yo

⋀ sk2p

Framed Lace

Knitted lace in fine weight yarn looks terrific when sandwiched between two panes of glass and inserted into a solid color frame. Your wallpaper or paint color will peek through the glass, so the background of your art will always be a perfect match to your décor. This piece is knit straight, so it's the perfect circle for knitters who don't like double-pointed needles!

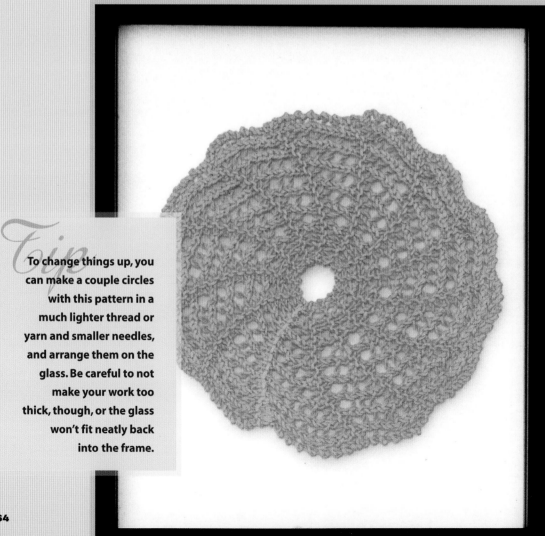

Tip

To change things up, you can make a couple circles with this pattern in a much lighter thread or yarn and smaller needles, and arrange them on the glass. Be careful to not make your work too thick, though, or the glass won't fit neatly back into the frame.

Finished Size

External measurement of frame is 12" x 15" (30.5 x 38 cm); finished knit circle is 9" (23 cm) in diameter

Materials

- Approximately 75 yd. (69 m) sport weight #3 yarn [shown in Premier Yarns Cotton Fair Solid; 52% cotton, 48% acrylic; 3.5 oz. (100 g), 317 yd. (290 m) per skein] 1 skein #2704 Turquoise
- U.S. size 6 (4 mm) knitting needles. Gauge is not critical for this pattern.
- Frame with two sheets of glass—frame shown is 12" x 15" (30.5 x 38 cm), but as long as the knitting fits inside you can use whatever size you like
- Tapestry needle

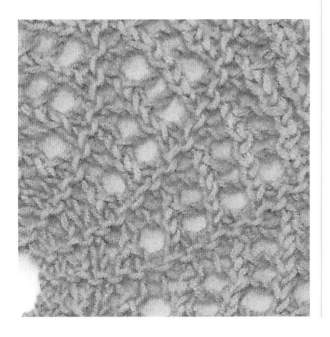

Lace Circle

Cast on 15 sts with long-tail cast-on.

Row 1 (WS): Knit.
Row 2 (RS): (K2tog, yo) 6 times, k1, turn—13 sts.
Row 3: P12, k1.
Row 4: (K2tog, yo) 5 times, k1, turn—11 sts.
Row 5: P10, k1.
Row 6: (K2tog, yo) 4 times, k1, turn—9 sts.
Row 7: P8, k1.
Row 8: (K2tog, yo) 3 times, k1, turn—7 sts.
Row 9: P6, k1.
Row 10: (K2tog, yo) twice, k1, turn—5 sts.
Row 11: P4, k1.
Row 12: K2tog, yo, k1, turn—3 sts.
Row 13: P2, k1.
Rows 14 and 15: Knit all sts—15 sts.
Rep Rows 2–15 eleven times more, then Rows 2–14 once.
Bind off knitwise.

Finishing

Sew bound-off edge to cast-on edge with tapestry needle.
Block into circular shape.
Weave in all ends.
Center blocked piece between sheets of glass and follow frame manufacturer's instructions for assembling the frame.

Abbreviations

Beg	begin(ning)
dec	decrease(ing)
DPN(s)	double-pointed needle(s)
k	knit
k2tog	knit 2 sts together
kfb	knit into the front and back of 1 st
LC	left cross
M1	make 1 increase
p	purl
RC	right cross
rep	repeat
RS	right side
sk2p	sl 1, k2tog, pass slipped st over knit st
sl	slip
ssk	slip, slip, knit
St st	stockinette stitch
st(s)	stitch(es)
WS	wrong side
wyib	with yarn in back
wyif	with yarn in front
yo	yarn over

Visual Index

Tab-Top Towel

2

Exfoliating Washcloth

4

Felted Soap Cover

6

Plush Bathmat

8

Lacy Mirror

10

Lined Basket

12

Lacy Pedicure
Socks

16

Pink Lace
Bathmat

20

Tray Liner

22

Shaped
Washcloths

25

Cabled Towels

30

Chevron
Washcloth

33

Textured Bath
Mitt

35

Slip Stitch
Trio of
Washcloths

38

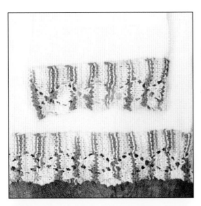

Edged Towels

44

Textured Linen
Washcloth

47

Diagonal
Washcloth

49

Storage Basket

51

Chenille Set

54

Faux Cable
Washcloth

60

Acorn Pattern
Washcloth

62

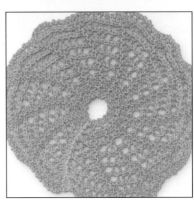

Framed Lace

64